Let's Recycle and Reuse!

by Becky Manfredini

 HOUGHTON MIFFLIN HARCOURT

PHOTOGRAPHY CREDITS: COVER ©Ariel Skelley/Blend Images/Corbis; 3 (b) ©Comstock/Jupiterimages/Getty Images; 4 (t) ©Greg Balfour Evans/Alamy Images; 5 (cr) ©Ashley Cooper/Corbis; 6 (br) SW Productions/Getty Images; 7 (tr) ©Ariel Skelley/Blend Images/Corbis; 8 (r) ©Photo Disc/ Getty Royalty Free; 9 (r) ©Pat Sullivan/AP Images; 10 (t) ©Michael Ventura/Alamy Images

Printed in U.S.A.

ISBN: 978-0-544-07296-1

3 4 5 6 7 8 9 10 1083 21 20 19 18 17 16 15 14

4500470116   A B C D E F G

Contents

Vocabulary	Stretch Vocabulary
natural resource	landfill
renewable resource	mulch
nonrenewable resource	sustainable
conservation	cullet

Introduction

Do you ever wonder where food, clothing, and homes come from? They come from where we live: Earth. Natural resources are useful materials that come from nature. Wood from trees is a natural resource that construction workers use to build homes.

Many materials people use are renewable resources, or resources that can be replaced. For example, workers chop down trees. Furniture makers use the wood to make chairs and tables. Then new trees are planted to replace the trees that were cut down.

Other resources people use are called nonrenewable resources because they can't be replaced. For example, some energy sources, such as coal, natural gas, and oil, can't be replaced. We have to use these resources wisely!

The fuel that many vehicles use is made from oil, a nonrenewable resource.

This water slide is made of molded plastic.

Plastic Is Everywhere!

What is strong, lightweight, and can be made into almost anything? The answer is plastic. Although plastic objects are made by people, the materials used to make plastic come from nature. Plastic is made from oil and natural gas, two nonrenewable resources.

The word "plastic" comes from the Greek word *plastikos*, meaning "moldable" or "formable." When plastic is heated, it turns into a liquid or semi-solid form. Then it can be molded into almost any shape. What do a toothbrush, traffic light, and football helmet have in common? These objects are made of plastic. Many people even have plastic inside their bodies. Certain kinds of medical implants are made of plastic.

Recycle Plastic Water Bottles

How can people make sure that nonrenewable resources don't disappear? They can use conservation methods, which are ways to save resources. One way is to use less of something to make its supply last longer.

One way to conserve oil and natural gas is to recycle plastic. Americans use about 2.5 million plastic bottles every hour. When Americans throw them away they end up in landfills, places where garbage is buried to dispose of it. Instead of throwing plastic bottles away, you can recycle them so they are turned into new products.

This landfill probably contains many plastic bottles that can be recycled rather than thrown away.

This sleeping bag contains fiberfill, a material created from recycled plastic bottles.

When Rubber Tires Get Tired

Did you know that rubber can be natural or synthetic? Some rubber comes from nature by way of the rubber tree. This kind of tree originated in Brazil. Today it is mainly grown in other tropical countries, such as Indonesia, Malaysia, and Thailand. Rubber can also be made artificially from oil, coal, and natural gas using a chemical process.

Whether a product is made with natural or synthetic rubber, it can sometimes wear down. For example, think about rubber tires. Cars use them. Buses use them. Your bike has a pair of them. But when the rubber wears thin, your tires become worn out. They get tired.

Some bicycle tires are made with synthetic rubber.

When tires are no longer useable, many people want to throw them away in landfills. However, because of their volume, tires take up a lot of space in landfills. Rubber tires are also difficult to break down.

Many tires are shredded and turned into other products. Shredded tires are used as mulch. Gardeners spread mulch around plants and trees to hold in moisture and prevent weeds from growing. Today, many playground surfaces

Old tires can be turned into tire swings.

are made from rubber to make them softer and safer to play on than concrete surfaces. Boat bumpers on docks, wallets, and even new tires are made of recycled rubber.

When we recycle tires, we reduce the amount of raw rubber needed to make new products. And we save oil and other nonrenewable resources.

Recycle Aluminum Cans

You and your family probably recycle many empty cans that were once filled with dog food, soup, or a drink. Some cans are aluminum. Place a magnet next to a can. If it doesn't attract the can, the can may be aluminum.

Aluminum is an important metal because its use is sustainable. Sustainable means we should be able to use the resource without running out of it—if we are careful and make good decisions.

People can recycle aluminum to use again and again. We use aluminum to make electrical equipment, jewelry, cooking utensils, and foil wrap. We use aluminum on the outside of houses to make them last a long time.

Aluminum foil is a useful product that people recycle so it can be made into a new product.

Did you know that aluminum cans are 100% recyclable? Just drop some in the recycling bin, and they might eventually be turned into a license plate for a car or other vehicle. Here's how it happens:

1. Workers take the cans to a factory.
2. After the cans are shredded, workers wash them. Then the cans are made into aluminum chips.
3. The chips are heated and melted. The liquid is poured into molds called ingots.
4. The ingots go to another factory, where they are heated again. When the ingots melt, they become flat sheets of aluminum.
5. License plates are cut out of the flat sheets of aluminum.
6. When the license plates are finished, they are sent to people to put on their cars.

Like soup cans, aluminum license plates are recycled again and again!

Workers sort, clean, crush, and melt glass after it is recycled.

From Jelly Jar to Drinking Glass

Another material that we can use again and again is glass. Factory workers combine natural materials, such as sand, soda ash, and limestone, to make glass.

How does a jelly jar become a drinking glass? First you put your jelly jars into a recycling bin. Then workers pick up the jars and bring them to a recycling center. There other workers sort the glass by color. Then machines wash the glass. When it is clean, the glass is crushed into small pieces called cullet. This broken, or waste, glass is melted along with new material. Then it is poured into molds and shaped into a drinking glass. Jewelry, tiles, countertops, vases, and stained glass windows are made of recycled glass.

Paper: Recycle and Reuse

Paper is everywhere. We write on it, print the news on it, and make egg cartons out of it. As you learned, paper comes from trees, a valuable and renewable natural resource. In 2010, Americans used about 71 million tons of paper products. They recycled an average of 334 pounds of paper per person.

You cannot recycle paper over and over forever. Each time it is recycled and turned into something new the fibers get shorter. After being recycled several times, the fibers can no longer bond together.

Before you recycle index cards or notebooks, think of ways to reuse them. You can use paper for an art project, shred it for packing material, or write on both sides of notebook paper.

Recycled paperboard is used to produce cardboard boxes.

From Soup Can to Pencil Holder

Besides recycling soup or juice cans, you can reuse them to make many things. Wash a can and paint it. Fill the can halfway with water, pick some flowers, and use it as a vase for a table. Or make a planter. Place soil in the can and plant some flowers. Water your flowers every day.

Another practical use for a can is to make a pencil holder. You can paint the can or put a scrap of wallpaper around it to cover the can. (Go to a local store and ask for free wallpaper samples.) Place pens, pencils, scissors, and other tools in your new and improved can.

You can use your imagination to decorate different kinds of cans and reuse them for different purposes.

Make a Milk Carton Bird Feeder

It's time to reuse a milk carton and care for some feathered friends. Ask an adult for help with any tricky step. Wear your safety goggles, too.

Reusing milk cartons instead of buying wooden birdfeeders can save a tree.

1. Clean out a milk carton.
2. Cut a large opening on two joining sides of the carton. Start about 3 inches from the bottom to make each opening.
3. Paint the carton with nontoxic paint. Let it dry.
4. Make a perch for the birds. Poke a pencil-size hole under each opening that you cut out. Insert a pencil or twig for the perch.
5. Fill the bottom of the feeder with birdseed.
6. Use string to hang the feeder on a tree branch.

Show You Care: Be Earth Aware

Think about what you have learned about how to care for Earth and all of its renewable and nonrenewable resources. Copy the chart below on to a piece of paper. Then keep track of everything that you reuse or recycle each day. Record each item on the chart. At the end of the week, discuss your results with other students in your class.

	Recycle	Reuse
Monday		
Tuesday		
Wednesday		
Thursday		
Friday		
Saturday		
Sunday		

Make a Reminder Pad!

People use notepaper and sticky notes to remind themselves to go to the store or do a chore. Think of a friend who uses them. Find scraps of paper that you haven't written on. Cut the paper into smaller pieces. Stack the paper together and tie a ribbon around it. Share your gift with a friend!

Write a Slogan

Encourage other students to reuse and recycle things instead of throwing them away. Write a slogan that reminds them to care about Earth. For example: *When in doubt, don't throw it out!* Draw a picture that illustrates your slogan and place it on the classroom bulletin board.

Glossary

conservation [kahn·ser·VAY·shuhn] The use of less of something to make its supply last longer.

cullet [KUL·let] Broken and crushed recycled glass gathered for melting purposes and made into new glass.

landfill [LAND·fil] A place where garbage is buried to dispose of it.

mulch [MUHLCH] A loose material that is spread around plants and trees to hold in moisture and prevent weeds from growing.

natural resource [NACH·er·uhl REE·sohrs] Anything from nature that people can use.

nonrenewable resource [nahn·ri·NOO·uh·buhl REE·sohrs] A resource that, once used, cannot be replaced in a reasonable amount of time.

renewable resource [ri·NOO·uh·buhl REE·sohrs] A resource that can be replaced within a reasonable amount of time.

sustainable [sus·TAYN·uh·buhl] Able to be continued without using up all the natural resource.